Savvy

GLOSS, FLOSS, and Wash

DIY CRAFTS AND RECIPES
for a Fresh Face and Teeth

by AUBRE
ANDRUS

CAPSTONE PRESS
a capstone imprint

Savvy Books are published by Capstone Press,
1710 Roe Crest Drive, North Mankato, Minnesota 56003
www.mycapstone.com

Library of Congress Cataloging-in-Publication Data
Names: Andrus, Aubre, author.
Title: Gloss, floss, and wash : DIY crafts and recipes for a fresh face and
teeth / by Aubre Andrus.
Description: North Mankato, Minnesota : Capstone Press, [2017] | Series:
Savvy. DIY Day Spa | Audience: Age 9-13. | Audience: Grade 4 to 6. |
Identifiers: LCCN 2016030043| ISBN 9781515734475 (library binding) |
ISBN 9781515734512 (eBook PDF)
Subjects: LCSH: Skin—Care and hygiene—Juvenile literature. | Face—Care
and hygiene—Juvenile literature. | Teeth—Care and hygiene—Juvenile
literature. | Handicraft—Juvenile literature.
Classification: LCC RL86 .A53 2017 | DDC 646.7/2—dc23
LC record available at https://lccn.loc.gov/2016030043

Editor: Eliza Leahy
Designer: Tracy McCabe
Creative Director: Heather Kindseth
Production Specialist: Katy LaVigne

Image Credits: Photographs by Capstone Studio: Karon Dubke,
photographer; Sarah Schuette, photo stylist; Marcy Morin,
studio scheduler; Author photo by Ariel Andrus

Printed and bound in the USA.
010062S17

TABLE OF CONTENTS

INTRODUCTION

Creating a spa experience at home is easier than you might think. Believe it or not, you'll find a lot of what you need in the kitchen. The recipes in this book aren't much different from traditional recipes (such as cupcakes, cookies, and cake), but these recipes aren't meant to be eaten. Instead of soothing your hunger, these recipes will give you a fresh face!

The skin on your face needs to be taken care of differently than the skin on the rest of your body. It's more delicate and comes with a set of problems such as acne, clogged pores, and dry or oily patches. These recipes will help balance your skin in a natural way. And don't worry, we didn't forget about your teeth. After all, your smile is the most important part of your face!

Flip through these pages to find your favorites in the same way you'd flip through a cookbook. There's no wrong or right place to start. There's a homemade spa product for everyone, from lotion to balms to sprays to masks. We even added some essential oils to these recipes so your DIY spa experience is as relaxing as the real thing.

Enjoy these products alone, give them as gifts, or invite some friends over for a spa party.

IT'S TIME TO PAMPER YOURSELF!

SPECIALTY INGREDIENTS

Some of the recipes in this book call for simple ingredients that you may already have in your kitchen, such as baking soda, olive oil, or vanilla extract. But there are some specialty ingredients that you likely won't find at home.

Luckily, they can be found at health food stores or organic grocery stores near the spices, pharmacy, or beauty aisles. You can also find them online. Here are some of those ingredients and the reasons you need them in your recipes.

aloe vera gel

shea butter

vegetable glycerin

Aloe Vera Gel – *Aloe vera gel moisturizes skin and hair, as well as soothes sunburn with a cooling effect.*

Beeswax — *Beeswax helps firm balms and creams. These recipes call for grated beeswax, which can be made by using a cheese grater on a bar of pure beeswax. Or you could buy beeswax pastilles, which are small granules or pellets.*

Coconut Oil – *Coconut oil moisturizes your skin and hair.*

Distilled Water – *Distilled water has been boiled to remove impurities, and it will help your ingredients last longer. It can be found at grocery stores.*

Jojoba Oil – *Jojoba oil is soothing when applied to skin, from acne to sunburn.*

Rosewater – *Rosewater soothes and strengthens skin, and it also conditions hair. It has a floral perfume-like aroma.*

Sea Salt – *The rough texture of sea salt helps exfoliate skin while naturally detoxifying.*

Shea Butter – *Shea butter moisturizes and balances skin without clogging pores. It can even help heal cuts and scrapes.*

Vegetable Glycerin – *Vegetable glycerin naturally attracts moisture when applied to skin.*

Witch Hazel – *Witch hazel soothes itchy or irritated skin, including acne and foot infections. It can also tighten and moisturize skin.*

ESSENTIAL OILS

Many of the recipes in this book call for essential oils. Essential oils are used for aromatherapy (they smell lovely and can make you feel great) and for health benefits for your hair, skin, and body.

They can be found at health food stores, organic grocery stores, or online. Here are the essential oils used in this book and the reasons you might use them in your recipes.

Lavender
Lavender is probably the most popular essential oil. It can soothe skin and possibly help fight acne. It has a floral aroma that can help you fall asleep.

Roman Chamomile
Roman chamomile essential oil soothes skin and has a calming aroma that can help you wind down and clear your sinuses.

Lemon*
Lemon essential oil is antibacterial. It can prevent infection when applied to the skin. Its citrus aroma is energizing.

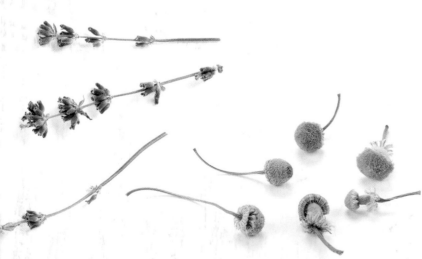

Peppermint

Peppermint essential oil has a cooling effect. It can relieve muscle pain and has an invigorating aroma that can make you feel alert.

Tea Tree

Tea tree oil fights bacteria, fungi, and viruses, so it can help treat athlete's foot, acne, and more when applied to the skin.

Be careful! Don't allow any undiluted essential oil to get on your skin or in your eyes or mouth. Recipes from this book containing essential oils should not be used on children under age 6, and for older children, an adult's help is recommended.

*Lemon essential oil could be phototoxic, which means it can make your skin extra-sensitive to the sun. Don't apply citrus essential oils to bare skin before going outside. And always wear sunscreen!

MEASURING YOUR INGREDIENTS

Essential oils are very potent and must be diluted with distilled water or a carrier oil, such as coconut oil, jojoba oil, or olive oil. It might not seem like you're using a lot, but a little goes a long way!

The recipes in this book dilute the essential oil to about 1 percent. That means some recipes require only a few drops. We measure essential oils by the drop in this book because it's hard to measure any other way. (There are 20 drops in 1 milliliter, and ¼ teaspoon is a little more than 1 milliliter.) There are very few recipes that will require more than ¼ teaspoon of essential oil.

coconut oil

jojoba oil

olive oil

HOW TO SAFELY MELT BUTTER AND OIL

Shea butter is a soft solid that must be melted for some recipes in this book. A double boiler is best for melting oils and butters, but you can also microwave them at 50 percent power in 30-second increments, stirring in between, until the solid is almost all the way melted. Stir to complete the melting process. You don't want to overheat the oils or butters.

Coconut oil is also used in this book. Whether your coconut oil is a solid or a liquid depends on where you live, what time of year it is, and the air temperature. To solidify it, place it in the refrigerator until it hardens. To liquefy it, heat it in a microwave-safe bowl in 10-second increments at 50 percent power, stirring in between, until the solid is almost all the way melted.

It's best to heat the solids in a microwave-safe bowl with a pourable spout and a handle, such as a glass Pyrex measuring cup. Be sure to always wear an oven mitt when removing a hot bowl from the microwave.

HOW TO SAFELY STORE YOUR PRODUCTS

It's best to use glass containers, not plastic, to store any recipe that contains essential oils, because the essential oils can deteriorate plastic over time. All of the recipes in this book make small batches since they are natural and don't contain preservatives.

Unless indicated otherwise, the finished products should be stored in a cool, dry place and should be used within two to four weeks. Never use a recipe if it looks like it has grown mold, if it has changed colors, or if it begins to smell bad.

ALLERGIES

Some people have skin sensitivities and allergies. Check with your doctor or dermatologist before using any of these recipes.

CLEAN UP

Many of the recipes in this book use oils and butters, which might feel greasy. To clean up, wipe your hands and any used dishes with a dry paper towel first, then use soap and water to wash. When using recipes in the bathtub, wipe the floor clean with a dry towel afterward. Oils and butters can make surfaces slippery and unsafe.

WHERE TO FIND PACKAGING FOR YOUR PRODUCTS

It's important to use brand new containers to store your products. It will help prevent mold from growing. Here's where you can buy containers that are perfect for the recipes in this book:

• reusable 2-ounce (59-milliliter) glass bottles or 4-ounce (118-mL) glass containers can be found in the essential oil aisle at health food stores

• reusable 2-ounce (59-mL) plastic spray bottles or 3-ounce (89-mL) plastic squeeze bottles can be found in the travel section of grocery or convenience stores

• reusable 4-ounce (118-mL) spice tins or empty spice jars can be found in the bulk spice aisle in grocery stores or health food stores

• half-pint glass jars can be found in the jam or canning aisle in grocery stores or health food stores

• round plastic containers with screw-top lids can be found in the jewelry or bead storage aisle at craft stores or in the travel aisle of department stores

Chocolate Mousse Face Mask

You will need:

1 tbsp (15 mL) honey
2 tsp (10 mL) cocoa powder
1 tsp (5 mL) jojoba oil or olive oil
¼ tsp (1.2 mL) fine sea salt

Would you like to order off the dessert menu? This cleansing chocolate mask will soothe breakouts, and it acts as a gentle exfoliating scrub when you rinse it off. To use, gently massage a thin layer onto face, avoiding eye area. Leave on for 10 minutes, then rinse off mask completely before patting face dry with a clean towel.

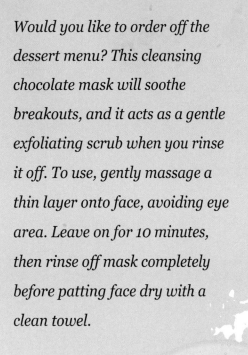

cocoa powder

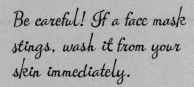

Be careful! If a face mask stings, wash it from your skin immediately.

DIRECTIONS:

Mix all ingredients together in a bowl. Stir until mixture forms a pudding-like paste. This recipe makes one mask.

Breakfast Face Mask

You will need:

- 1 tsp (5 mL) powdered milk
- 1 tsp (5 mL) honey
- 3 tsp (15 mL) plain yogurt

You can eat your breakfast and wear it too! This mask combines milk, honey, and yogurt to form a calming and cooling mask you'll love. To use, gently massage a thick layer onto face, avoiding eye area. Leave on for 10 minutes, then rinse off mask completely before patting face dry with a clean towel.

yogurt

powdered milk

Be careful! If any face mask ever stings, wash it from your skin immediately.

DIRECTIONS:

Mix powdered milk, honey, and yogurt in a small bowl.
Stir until mixture forms a paste. This recipe makes one mask.

Rosewater Toner

You will need:

¼ cup (60 mL) rosewater
2 tbsp (30 mL) witch hazel
¼ tsp (1.2 mL) vegetable glycerin

This natural toner tightens and moisturizes your skin. It's great to put on before heading to bed. To use, first clean your face, then apply toner with a cotton ball. Shake before each use, and avoid contact with your eyes.

vegetable glycerin

rosewater

DIRECTIONS:

Mix ingredients in a bowl with a pourable spout. Pour mixture into a lidded container. Makes enough to fill a 3-ounce (89-mL) bottle.

Cooling Facial Refresher Spray

You will need:

¼ cup (60 mL) aloe vera gel
5 drops peppermint essential oil
¼ tsp (1.2 mL) witch hazel

Aloe vera gel and peppermint essential oil create a cooling effect, which can provide temporary relief from sunburns or hot days. Shake before use, and avoid contact with your eyes by covering them with your hand or a washcloth. Store in the refrigerator to keep spray extra cool.

aloe vera gel

DIRECTIONS:

Mix all ingredients in a bowl with a pourable spout. Pour into a 2-ounce (59-mL) spray bottle.

Eye Pillow

You will need:

1 clean knee sock
1 cup (240 mL) dry rice
10 drops lavender essential oil (optional)

The lavender in this mask has a calming effect, and the cooling sensation can help soothe puffy eyes. Place in the freezer for a few hours, then rest the pillow across your eyes for 15 minutes. It can also be warmed in the microwave* for 30 seconds. Make a few extra to share with friends!

DIRECTIONS:

Pour rice into a bowl with a pourable spout. Add essential oil and stir. Before you pour the mixture into the sock, tie a knot at the toe end of the sock. Then pour the rice mixture into the sock while holding sock over a bowl to catch any spills. Leave about 3 inches (7.5 centimeters) of sock on the end. Then form a knot, and pull tightly. Replace rice and lavender oil every 6 months—or sooner if the fragrance begins to fade.

* If you microwave the eye mask, be sure to check the temperature of it with the back of your hand before putting it on your eyes.

Vanilla Coffee Lip Scrub

You will need:

- ¼ cup (60 mL) sugar
- 1 tsp (5 mL) ground coffee
- 1 tbsp (15 mL) olive oil
- 1 tsp (5 mL) vanilla extract

Chapped lips? No problem! A good scrub can flake away any dead skin and reveal your healthy lips. While standing over a sink, use your finger to scoop out a small amount. Then rub it onto your lips in a circular motion. Rinse off excess. This makes your lips feel great, and it tastes good too!

sugar

DIRECTIONS:

Mix the ingredients together in a small bowl. Scoop a portion into a small, circular storage container with screw-top lid. This recipe makes about 5 portions.

Coconut Lip Balm

You will need:

2 tbsp (30 mL) coconut oil
2 tbsp (30 mL) grated beeswax
   or beeswax pastilles
4 tsp (20 mL) olive oil

Making lip balm is easier than you might think. Coconut oil and olive oil can serve as natural lip healing remedies on their own, but we're going to mix them together to create a nourishing blend.

coconut oil

beeswax pastilles

DIRECTIONS:

Scoop beeswax and coconut oil into a microwave-safe bowl with a pourable spout. Microwave in 30-second increments at 50 percent power, stirring each time, until mixture mostly liquefies. Remove bowl with an oven mitt and stir until clear, not cloudy. Add olive oil and stir.

Carefully pour into small, clear, circular storage containers with screw-top lids. Let harden at room temperature, then screw on caps. This recipe makes about six lip balms.

Warming Lemon Honey Face Wash

You will need:

3 tbsp (45 mL) honey
3 tbsp (45 mL) vegetable glycerin
3 drops lemon essential oil

Sensitive skin? This natural face wash smells sweet and will keep your skin looking bright and soft while fighting off acne. Honey is antibacterial, which means it's a great cleanser, and it helps heal your skin. This face wash won't produce suds, but don't worry—it's working! To use, gently massage a small amount in circular motions onto your dry face. It will warm naturally as you rub it onto your skin. Rinse with warm water, then pat dry with a clean towel.

Tip: Raw unfiltered honey can be found at natural food stores and may have more benefits for your skin than processed honey.

DIRECTIONS:

Stir all ingredients in a bowl with a pourable spout. Pour into a plastic squeeze bottle or tube. This recipe makes enough to fill a 3-ounce (89-mL) bottle.

Skin-Soothing Spray

You will need:

2 tbsp (30 mL) aloe vera gel

4 tbsp (60 mL) rosewater

3 drops Roman chamomile essential oil
(optional)

Hydrate and soften your skin with this ultra-calming spray that smells good too. Shake before each use, and avoid contact with your eyes by covering them with your hand or a washcloth.

aloe vera gel

DIRECTIONS:

Mix all ingredients in a bowl with a pourable spout. Pour into a glass spray bottle. This recipe makes enough to fill a 2-ounce (59-mL) spray bottle.

Exfoliating Face Scrub

You will need:

    3 tsp (15 mL) baking soda
    2 tsp (10 mL) jojoba oil

Give your skin a gentle scrub with this baking soda-based mix. To use, gently massage a small amount in circular motions onto your dry face. Rinse with warm water, then pat dry with a clean towel.

jojoba oil

DIRECTIONS:

Mix all ingredients in a small bowl. This recipe makes enough for a single use.

DIY Scented Sprays

This spray doesn't go directly on your face, but on your pillow! Sometimes a whiff of a sweet scent can make you instantly feel better. These sprays can help energize or calm you. They also can be great gifts to give to friends.

Dreamy Pillow Mist

To look your best, you need your beauty sleep! This pillow mist will help lull you to dreamland thanks to a calming blend of lavender and chamomile. Shake before each use.

You will need:

3 tbsp (45 mL) distilled water

1 tsp (5 mL) witch hazel

5 drops lavender essential oil

10 drops Roman chamomile essential oil

Citrus Linen Spray

Your pillows and sheets will smell fresh and clean, thanks to the deodorizing and energizing lemon scent in this linen spray. This can be used as a room spray too, and it's especially perfect for early mornings. Shake before each use.

You will need:

3 tbsp (45 mL) distilled water

1 tsp (5 mL) witch hazel

15 drops lemon essential oil

DIRECTIONS:

Mix all ingredients in a bowl with a pourable spout. Pour into a spray bottle. Each recipe makes enough to fill a 2-ounce (59-mL) container.

Face Lotions

The ingredients in these recipes have low comedogenic ratings, which means they are less likely to clog your pores. Shea butter and jojoba oil might feel greasy, but both ingredients are exceptional ways to nourish, moisturize, and heal your skin. To use, massage a small amount onto your face and neck. Remember, a little goes a long way!

Calming Face Lotion

This lotion will soothe your skin as well as soothe your mind thanks to the calming scent.

You will need:

¼ cup (60 mL) shea butter
¼ cup (60 mL) jojoba oil
10-15 drops lavender essential oil

Acne-Fighting Face Lotion

This lotion will moisturize while healing and preventing acne—without drying out your skin.

You will need:

¼ cup (60 mL) shea butter
¼ cup (60 mL) jojoba oil
10-15 drops tea tree essential oil

DIRECTIONS:

Scoop shea butter into a microwave-safe mixing bowl. Microwave in 30-second increments at 50 percent power, stirring each time, until it mostly liquefies. Remove bowl with an oven mitt and stir until clear, not cloudy. Add jojoba oil and stir.

To turn the liquid into a cream, cover the bowl with plastic wrap and place in the refrigerator until the texture resembles softened butter (this step should take no longer than one hour). Add essential oil, then whip with a hand mixer on low speed for 3-5 minutes or until the color brightens and peaks form.

When desired consistency is reached, scoop into a lidded glass jar with a spatula. Makes about ½ cup (120 mL).

Soothing Face Wipes

You will need:
extra virgin olive oil
cotton rounds (makeup
    remover pads)
small jar

Olive oil is a safe and easy way to get your face squeaky clean—it even removes makeup, including mascara. Olive oil moisturizes your skin as it cleans, and it will leave your face feeling incredibly smooth. To use, gently massage the wipe across your face and neck. Rinse with warm water, then pat dry.

olive oil

DIRECTIONS:

Stack seven cotton rounds in a small jar. Pour a small amount of olive oil into the jar, covering each cotton round. The cotton rounds should be damp, not soaked. This recipe makes enough face wipes for one week.

Minty Homemade Toothpaste

You will need:

- ⅓ cup (80 mL) coconut oil
- ⅓ cup (80 mL) baking soda
- ¼ tsp (1.2 mL) Stevia extract powder for sweetness (optional)
- 10 drops peppermint essential oil

coconut oil

baking soda

To use, scoop a small amount of paste onto your toothbrush. The paste will melt in your mouth as you brush. Brush your teeth for two minutes, then spit and rinse. Do not swallow the toothpaste.

DIRECTIONS:

Melt coconut oil in microwavable-safe bowl in 10-second increments at 50 percent power, stirring in between. Remove from microwave with oven mitt. Stir in baking soda and Stevia.

To turn the liquid into a paste, cover the bowl with plastic wrap and place in the refrigerator until the liquid resembles softened butter (this step should take no longer than one hour). Add essential oil, then whip with a hand mixer on low speed for 3-5 minutes, or until the color brightens and peaks form. Store in a lidded container in a cool, dry place.

Peppermint Mouthwash

You will need:

- 4 tbsp (60 mL) distilled water
- ¼ tsp (1.2 mL) baking soda
- ⅛ tsp (0.6 mL) salt
- ⅛ tsp (0.6 mL) Stevia extract powder for sweetness (optional)
- 1-2 drops peppermint essential oil

If you wear braces, it can be hard to clean your teeth completely. Mouthwashes can help! Shake the bottle before each use, then pour a small amount into a cup. Swish in your mouth for 30 seconds, then spit into sink. Do not swallow.

salt

Peppermint

DIRECTIONS:

Mix all ingredients in a bowl with a pourable spout. Pour into a lidded bottle. Makes enough to fill a 2-ounce (59-mL) bottle. Store in a cool, dry place.

PRETTY PACKAGING

All of your lotions, potions, and sprays look and smell amazing, but since they're homemade, the jars they're in are often boring. Not only will these labeling ideas help beautify your beauty products, they'll help you remember what's what!

Simple Stickers

Use letter stickers (found at craft stores) to spell out what's inside. Letter stickers come in all shapes and sizes, including glitter versions, so mix and match to create a unique look for each product.

Lovely Labels

Adhesive sticker paper, which you can find in office supply stores, is the easiest way to make great labels in all sizes. Design a logo or a label on your computer and print it out on adhesive paper, or just draw your own directly on the adhesive paper with colored pens or markers. Cut out your designs when you're done and attach to the front or the lid of your product.

Top It Off

If you're using mason jars to store your products, the top screws off in two pieces. Trace the circle portion onto a piece of paper. Write your product name with markers or stickers. Cut out and apply to lid with double-sided tape. Patterned washi tape can be applied to the edge of the screw portion to finish the look.

CONGRATS TO YOU!

You've made all-natural recipes that beautify your mind and body. Which one was your favorite? The calming or the rejuvenating? The scrubbing or the soothing?

It's important to pamper yourself every week—if not every day. Taking even just five minutes to relax with one of your favorite recipes can relieve stress, calm your nerves, and help you find focus.

Once you've spoiled yourself, don't forget to share the love by giving away these beauty products as gifts. Or throw a party and pamper your guests with spa-like treatments.

It's all about feeling beautiful in the skin you're in. When you feel beautiful, you look beautiful!

READ MORE

Bolte, Mari. *Spa Projects You Can Make and Share.* Sleepover Girls Crafts. North Mankato, Minn.: Capstone, 2015.

Kenney, Karen Latchana. *Skin Care & Makeup Tips & Tricks.* Style Secrets. Minneapolis: Lerner Publications, 2016.

Shoket, Ann. *Seventeen Ultimate Guide to Beauty: The Best Hair, Skin, Nails & Makeup Ideas For You.* Philadelphia: Running Press, 2012.

Titles in this set:

 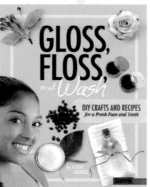  

ABOUT THE AUTHOR

Aubre Andrus is an award-winning children's book author with books published by Scholastic, American Girl, and more. She cherishes her time spent as the Lifestyle Editor of *American Girl* magazine where she developed crafts, recipes, and party ideas for girls. When she's not writing, Aubre loves traveling around the world, and some of her favorite places include India, Cambodia, and Japan. She currently lives in Los Angeles with her husband. You can find her website at www.aubreandrus.com.